Dedicated to John and Linda for making these books possible.

Content

Animals
Books
Disorders
Food and Drink
Games
History
Human Body
Inventions
Law
Miscellaneous
Movies
Music
People
Places
Religion
Science
Shakespeare
Technology
Video Games
War
Weapons
Words

ANIMALS

1. **Panthers exist.**
    A panther isn't a specific animal. A panther is any cat that can roar (tigers, lions, and jaguars.)
    Most people picture Bagheera from The Jungle Book when they think of a panther.
    Bagheera is a black leopard. Black leopards have spots but they are very hard to distinguish.

2. **Dolly the sheep was the first cloned animal.**
    The first cloned animal was a sea urchin in 1885, over a century before Dolly.
    Dolly wasn't even the first cloned sheep. The same institute that cloned her cloned five other sheep (two of which survived to adulthood.)
    The reason why Dolly was important was she was cloned from adult cells.
    The other sheep were cloned from embryos.

3. **Bugs Bunny is a rabbit.**
    Bugs is a hare. Technically, he's a fictitious, animated character but you know what I mean.

4. **The Easter Bunny is a rabbit.**
    He's a hare too (and also fictitious.)

5. Vultures are irredeemably disgusting animals.

Vultures eat 70% of all dead meat in the African regions where they live. Most people know vultures loom around dying animals, and pounce on them when they die. Because of this, disease doesn't have a chance to spread. Without vultures, there would be many more carcasses lying around Africa contaminating water.

Not only are vultures immune to rabies, anthrax, salmonella, and cholera, but their bodies don't spread the diseases; it expunges them.

Africa would be an ecological catastrophe without vultures.

6. Bats get caught in people's hair.

The most common place to be attacked by a bat is the toe. Since bats rely on sound waves, walking will make the bat attracted to your feet because your feet make sounds with every step you take (and every move you make.)

7. Bats are horrible creatures.

Bats are the most efficient animals in the world at killing insects. One bat can kill six hundred insects in an hour. That's one insect dead every six seconds. Do you know how many insects there would be if bats didn't exist? (The answer is a lot.)

8.   A duck's quack doesn't echo.
If that was true (which it isn't,) who cares? How does this affect your life? I just had to include this because I have an image of a duck in a laboratory with scientists with clipboards who spent millions to see if a duck's quack echoes. How is this for the good of mankind?

9.   Don't kill a spider! Put it outside.
The reason the spider is inside is because it has adapted to the heat indoors. Once you chuck it outside, it dies within minutes. So if you thought you were a good person because you were putting spiders outside instead of squashing them, you were killing them anyway, only more slowly. Well done.

10.   Black widows are the most dangerous spiders in the world.
Black widows are predators and their prey are other insects. A black widow will never go out of its way to bite a human.

Bites are rare. Lethal bites are unheard of nowadays.

11.   The daddy longlegs is the most venomous spider but it has no teeth.
There is no such thing as a daddy longlegs. There are lots of spiders that have long legs but

there is no definitive spider with this appearance. Some daddy longlegs have venom but not enough to harm a human.

12.   Spiders...are evil.
Most spiders kill animals we hate like flies, bees, and mosquitoes. One spider can kill 2,000 insects a year.

But what about venomous spiders? There are 40,000 types of spider. Twelve of them are dangerous. Most spiders aren't strong enough for their bite to breach human skin.

13.   Spider webs are weak.
It's true that you could effortlessly destroy a web with your hand. But that's because the web strands are thin. If steel and spider silk were the same weight and size, the silk would be five times stronger.

14.   Spiders kill people.
The last recorded human death caused by a spider was in 1981 from a Sydney Funnel Web Spider in Australia.

15.   Animals can smell your fear.
An animal can't smell if you're afraid or not, but all animals can smell the fear of the same species (including humans.)

16. If you come across a crocodile, you are as good as dead.

The crocodile has the most powerful bite in the animal kingdom. I have seen a video of a crocodile chewing through a car like butter.

But because its muscles are so strong at clamping down, the muscles that open its mouth are extremely weak.

If a two-year old toddler put his or her fingers around a crocodile's mouth, a crocodile wouldn't be able to open it. A crocodile can be defeated with an elastic band wrapped around its snout.

17. Alligators live in the sewers under New York City.

Nature writer, Diana Ackerman said, "Alligators can only live in temperatures between 78 to 90 degrees Fahrenheit. That's 25-30 Celsius. They couldn't survive in a sewer, because they can't live in salmonella, shigella or E. coli."

18. The horse inspired the unicorn.

Bizarrely, the unicorn myth originated from the skeleton of a narwhal whale. During the crusades, knights stumbled upon an enormous horned skeleton and thought it was of a gigantic horned horse. This was a common belief until the seventeenth century.

Except there's one problem with the narwhal horn...

19. Narwhals have horns.

Horns have bone cartilage. The narwhal's "horn" has none.

Okay....if it's not a horn, what is it then?

It's a tooth. It starts in the whale's mouth but it keeps growing. Eventually it pierces through the poor whale's head. It is known as an "erupted tooth."

You may be thinking, "How is that practical?"

Teeth have millions of nerve-endings, which make them hypersensitive. A narwhal's erupted tooth is so sensitive that it can tell if it is approaching salt water or non-salt water. Narwhals can't survive in fresh water so this erupted tooth is evolution's way of keeping them alive.

20. Rhino's horns are made of bone.

No, and just in case you think you are clever, it's not hair either. It's keratin, the same thing your nails are made of.

There was a rhino with a horn made of bone called the Brontotheres 45 million years ago.

If the animal collided with a predator, the horn would shatter. The Brontotheres would be in agony with a broken face that would take months to heal. This impracticality led to its extinction.

If the modern-day rhino's horn breaks, it doesn't hurt and it heals much faster than bone.

21. Rhino's have horns.

A horn isn't just a pointy spike sticking out of an animal's head.

A horn by definition is a natural protruding point that has a bone core (which you know from the fact above a rhino doesn't have.)

22. Rhinos "horns" are used as aphrodisiac.

The "horn" has never been used as an aphrodisiac. It's used to deter a fever. It doesn't work. This idea stems from superstition rather than science.

23. Possums play dead.

If a possum sees a predator, it will seize up and become stiff like a board. The predator assumes it is dead and will not be interested in eating it (unless it's a vulture.)

Possums "don't play dead." It's not a conscious decision. They are so terrified, that their body goes into shock. Saying a possum "plays dead" is like saying a human "plays a heart attack" when they are terrified.

24. Turkeys come from North America.
No, and it's not Turkey either.
Despite their association with Thanksgiving, turkeys originally came from Mexico.

25. Camels are most common in the Middle East.
Camels are mostly found in Australia. They are so common, Saudi Arabia import them. Saudi Arabia also imports sand from Australia. Seriously.

26. Camels store water in their hump.
A camel's hump stores fat. Camels tend to get a reputation for how long they can go without water. A camel can only live about two weeks without water. The kangaroo rat can live the longest without water, which is five years.

27. People have always known that mosquitos are humanity's biggest killers.
Less than a hundred years ago, our ancestors believed that malaria was simply "bad air." It was believed that malaria was something you just "got" like the flu until as recently as the 1930s.

28. Buzzing mosquitoes cause malaria.
Only the silent mosquitos can infect you with malaria.

29.   If you touch a bird's nest, the mother bird will pick up on your scent and abandon its young.

Most birds can barely smell. Even if the mother bird saw you, it would not be enough reason to desert their offspring.

30.   The animal that has saved the most lives is the Saint Bernard.

The horseshoe crab has saved the most human lives.

These crabs (even though it's more like a spider) have blood that clots around invading bacteria and viruses.

This is used to test every single pharmaceutical drug. So every pill, injection, transfusion, and anesthetic you have ever had is all thanks to the horseshoe crab.

31.   Saint Bernard's used to carry small barrels of brandy on their collar.

This would weigh down the St. Bernard, slowing it down (last thing you need when someone is dying in the cold.)

This isn't even hypothetically possible. Brandy freezes quickly. Even if it didn't, alcohol makes you feel warmer, but your body gets colder so it would be counter-productive.

32. All oysters lay pearls.
If they did, pearls would be pretty worthless because they would be so common. The chances of a pearl forming are a thousand to one.

33. If a dangerous animal is about to attack you, you can distract it by pointing at something.
Only apes and elephants understand what pointing means.
If a bear was about to attack you and you pointed somewhere, the bear would just stare at your pointed finger. It might even think you are presenting something to the bear making it more encouraged to come towards you.

34. When the English originally came to Australia, they asked an Aborigine what a kangaroo was called. The Aborigine said, "I don't know" in his native tongue, which is "kangaroo."
Ladies and gentlemen, I give you the most interesting fact ever...that is completely not true.

35. Chimpanzees have more hair than humans.
Chimps have thicker hair but humans have more hair follicles.

36. Don't throw rice at weddings. If a bird eats it, it will explode.

The rice is dangerous to humans. It can easily catch in someone's eye. Throwing rice at a flat, slippery surface or on a stairs makes it likely that somebody would slip. But it would make their wedding more memorable. Hospitals have a tendency to do that.

37. Pandas only eat bamboo.

Pandas are slow, clumsy, and lethargic so bamboo is pretty easy prey. They would prefer to eat small animals to give them energy. Bamboo barely gives them enough energy to keep going.

38. Bees die when they sting you.

A bee's stinger can get stuck in a person's skin and the bee has to rip itself apart to escape.

If the bee is careful, or doesn't sting you at a funny angle, it will be fine.

So when people say, "You got stung, but at least the bee is dead," just remember that those people are liars.

39. The best thing to use for bee stings is butter.

Butter will numb the pain but it won't get rid of the bee sting in your skin.

The best thing to do is wipe the area with a credit card. Doctors do this in emergencies where people have been stung hundreds of times.

40. All bees live in hives.
85% of bees live alone. They don't live in a beehive or with a colony.

41. All bees make honey.
20% of bees make honey.

42. Bees shouldn't be able to fly aerodynamically.
A bee seems to be too big compared to its wings to be able to fly. No one knew how bees flew until 2005.

As HD technology advanced, bees wings could be studied in slow motion and high definition while it is flying. It turns out bees flap their wings 230 times per second, which is far more than other insects. Their wings don't just move up and down. They move with short choppy strokes, followed by a quick rotation of the wing as it spins over and reverses direction along with a very fast wing-beat frequency.

If you can't understand this, just pretend the explanation is, "Magic."

43. Wolverines aren't real.
Even Hugh Jackman didn't know wolverines existed until after he was cast in X-Men as Wolverine.

The wolverine is a small Canadian weasel that doesn't like confrontation.

If it is cornered, it becomes vicious and goes for the jugular vein, killing its predator almost instantly.

44. The elephant is the only mammal that can't jump.
An adult elephant can't jump but a young one can. The only mammals that can't jump at all are hippos and sloths.

45. A snake dislocates its jaw to eat a big animal.
It doesn't. Snakes just has an incredibly flexible jaw.

46. White horses don't exist.
They are very rare but there are pure white horses in the world.

47. Lobsters are red.
Lobsters are red after you cook them. Most lobsters are blue so it's hard for predators to see them underwater.

48.   The most ferocious animal is the lion.
   The honey badger is the most ferocious animal on Earth. It's not a badger but a weasel, like the wolverine. As you may guess, weasels ferocity is vastly underestimated.
   Honey badgers have no fear. Literally. They are immune to fear. Honey badgers have killed hyenas, crocodiles, bears, lions, tigers, and even humans. They have killed porcupines in spite of being horrendously stung. They've penetrated tortoise's hard shell through pure force. They even attack bees! What kind of animal is so psychotic that it would attack bees?!?!!
   Honey badgers can kill and eat venomous snakes in fifteen minutes.
   So what is the honey badgers ultimate advantage? How does it win against animals a hundred times its size? It goes for one body part. The reproductive organs. A honey badger can instantly tell where these organs are on any animal. Once this area has been attacked (or removed,) it doesn't matter how big an animal is; the honey badger is going to win.

49.   "Species" is another word for an animal.
   "Species" and "animals" aren't the same thing. A species is an animal that can have children that are fertile.

If a male lion mates with a female tiger, she will have a liger.

If a female lion mates with a male tiger, she will have to a tion.

Tions and ligers are animals but they aren't species because they can't produce young. If a tion mates with a lion, a tiger, a tion or a liger, it will never have offspring.

BOOKS

50. Winnie the Pooh is called Winnie the Pooh.
   His original name was Edward Bear.

51. Sherlock Holmes uses the art of deduction to solve crimes.
   Sherlock only ever uses abductive reasoning to solve crimes (using observation to make guesses and theories.) That is the complete opposite of deduction, which uses solid facts.
   Abductive reasoning is the least likely method to come to accurate conclusions.

52. Sherlock's love interest was Irene Adler.
   Irene said one sentence to Sherlock in the story, A Scandal in Bohemia. They had no romance. The author described Sherlock as being incapable of romance.

53. Sherlock Holmes is middle-aged.
   Holmes and Watson are in their twenties.

54.   Sherlock Holmes wears a deerstalker cap and smokes a calabash pipe.
   This cap and pipe was created for plays portraying Sherlock. These are not part of Sherlock's outfit in the books.

55. James Bond is a secret agent.
A British agent is an informant. Informants don't get engage in shooting assassins or fighting sumo wrestlers like Bond. What James Bond does would make him an Intelligence Officer.

56. James Bond always drinks vodka martini; shaken, not stirred.
Bond drinks whiskey more than any drink in Ian Fleming's books. He drinks triple whiskey 101 times in the novels.

57. In the book Dracula, sunlight is lethal to a vampire.
There is no mention of sunlight weakening or killing vampires.

In fact, there are eight references to Dracula chillaxing in the daytime.

58. Dracula is killed with a stake to the heart.
Dracula is killed by good old-fashioned decapitation.

59. The Monster in the Frankenstein novel looks just like the movie - green skin, square forehead and neck bolts.
The square forehead and bolts were created for the movie.

In the novel, the Monster is yellow.

60. The Monster in Frankenstein is resurrected with a lightning strike.

The book never explains how the Monster is resurrected.

61. The Monster in Frankenstein is a mute imbecile.

He is articulate and intelligent and teaches himself to speak by reading Paradise Lost.

62. In the Wizard of Oz, Dorothy has ruby shoes.

In the original novel by L. Frank Baum, The Wonderful Wizard of Oz, Dorothy's shoes were silver. They were changed to ruby for the movie as the colour would look better onscreen.

63. Moby Dick is a fictional story.

The author, Herman Melville based Moby Dick on a real albino whale called Mocha that attacked a ship in 1820, killing the crew.

Mocha's description is identical to Moby. Mocha made a sound when he sprayed his spout, which sounded like a roar as it is described in the novels.

He was covered in barnacles, ropes, and harpoons from whalers who had failed to kill him, just like Moby. Although the exact circumstances aren't identical to the book, it is "inspired by true events" more than most modern Hollywood movies.

64. Jeeves is a butler character in…something.

The name Jeeves is associated with a butler. It comes from the Jeeves and Wooster books. In these stories, Reginald Jeeves is the head of staff, a valet, but above all, NOT a butler.

DISORDERS

65.   Nicotine causes cancer.
Nicotine creates the addiction to smoking. The tar in a cigarette causes cancer.

66.   The radiation from a cellphone can cause cancer.
The radiation emitted from cellphones spreads so wide and thin, that it is harmless to humans.

67.   Sweat out a cold.
Putting a blanket on top of your head over a bowl of hot water feels nice but is utterly ineffective against a cold.

68.   Starve a fever.
Why would this work?! Food = fuel. Food = energy. Food = strength. You need strength to combat a fever. The more you eat, the stronger your immune system will be to fight the fever.

69.   Obsessive Compulsive Disorder makes you super clean.
People who suffer OCD have odd obsessions or habits (which they usually call rituals.) These rituals might be an inability to sit in blue chairs, the need to open and close every door three

times before leaving a room, or the need to clean a kitchen an incredibly specific way. Many OCD sufferers have rituals, which do not include over-cleanliness.

70. You can catch a cold by kissing someone with a cold.

The cold virus is in the nasal mucus, not the lips or tongue. Unless you kiss the inside of their nose, you should be fine.

71. You can get the flu from a flu-shot.

The flu-shot doesn't contain a weakened version of flu, as many people believe. It is impossible to catch the flu from this shot.

72. The best cure for depression is prescription drugs.

Many depressives say that a long walk can be just as effective as prescription drugs.

Placebos can be better than a drug designed to alleviate depression because the belief that it will help can be enough to alleviate your mood. Placebos can be more effective because you won't suffer side effects that most prescription drugs offer.

This isn't a generalization. Tests were carried out by Dr Arif Khan over a period of seventeen years. He found that placebos were successful in one-third of his patients. Prescription drugs worked on one-quarter of his patients (at most.)

73. Having depression means that you are really really sad.

When people say they're depressed because they had a bad day at work or they got dumped, what they are experiencing is nothing compared to depression.

If you have experienced a trauma or a death, you can experience incredible fear and sadness but not necessarily depression. Some people will never experience clinical depression in their entire life.

Depression is a clinical disorder. You can't just "get it." Nor can you stop having it. You need to use medication to regulate it.

The best way to differentiate between depression and sadness is this – you can snap out of sadness. You can't snap out of depression. If you lost somebody close to you and you were distraught, you would have to be strong for the sake of your family and friends and loved ones.

You can't do that with depression. You can't just pull through with willpower and mental strength. Depressives aren't just sad. It's a mental condition, one that never becomes easy to live with.

74. AIDS is a death sentence.
Thanks to advances in medicine, the average person infected with AIDS will live to sixty-nine.

75. Gay men are the most likely people to carry the AIDS virus.
The most common carriers of AIDS are heterosexual women between the ages of 18-25.

76. All deaf people use sign language.
Only 10% of deaf people use sign language. It's not as practical as you may assume. There is no definitive sign language. The American version of sign language is completely different to the English version.

A friend of mine's has a deaf mother called Sarah who knows sign language. Sarah's friend Maggie, lost her hearing and her hand years ago, which means Maggie can only sign with one hand. So Sarah uses a different type of sign language when talking to Maggie with one hand than when she talks to her other deaf friends. She basically had to learn a different language just to talk to ONE person!

And she usually can't speak to a deaf person who's foreign because their sign language is different to hers.

77. Deaf people read lips.

Less than a third of deaf people read lips. Deaf people actually read lips better when the person they are talking to doesn't know they are deaf.

When you speak to a deaf person, it's instinctive to over pronounce words and overuse your facial muscles which is not natural and it will make it less likely a deaf person will understand what you are trying to say.

Even the best lip readers don't pick up on every word. Their brain just can't process that much information that quickly and the person they are speaking with may be mumbling, mispronouncing words or have a heavy accent.

My friend Nathan lip-reads and he says it's like when you speak on the phone and the signal is bad. You can only hear some of the words but you know what the other person is saying.

78. Blind people can't see anything.

There are many types of blindness all showing variances in limited sight.

Legally blind is classified as having 10% eyesight or less.

Or to put it another way, the inability to read anything on the sight board (the one with the big E) in the opticians.

79.   All blind people read braille.
18% of blind people read through braille. Audiotapes are waaaaaaay easier than learning braille.

80.   People with Asperger's syndrome are socially inept and can't achieve anything in life.
The following people were diagnosed with Asperger's –

Paddy Considine, Susan Boyle, Jane Austen, Michael Palin, Steven Spielberg, Carl Jung, Alexander Graham Bell, Michelangelo, Woody Allen, Hans Christian Anderson, Charles Darwin, Isaac Asimov, Beethoven, George Orwell, Thomas Edison, Bobby Fischer, Henry Ford, Alfred Hitchcock, Jim Henson, Bob Dylan, Andy Kaufman, Mozart, Andy Warhol, Isaac Newton, Albert Einstein, Bill Gates, and American President and forger of the Declaration of Independence, Thomas Jefferson.

FOOD AND DRINK

81. Carrots are orange.
What we know now as a carrot has been heavily mutated over time. 5,000 years ago, carrots originally came from Afghanistan and they were purple and the inside of them was yellow.

82. Carrots improve your eyesight.
This idea came from RAF pilot, John "Cat Eyes" Cunningham who got his nicknames because he could spot enemy planes at nighttime with perfect accuracy. In an interview, he mentioned that he loved carrots and marketers saw it as an opportunity to sell them. The two aren't connected.

83. Oranges are orange.
Oranges are green. I don't mean like how bananas are green, but when they are ripe, they're yellow.

Oranges are naturally green in most countries. It's only orange in certain climates but most oranges worldwide stay green (but orange on the inside.)

When oranges were originally transported to Europe, the climate changed their color from green to orange. Europeans had never seen oranges before and assumed they were supposed to be orange.

The oranges you eat are made orange as most people wouldn't eat them, worried that they have gone off or they wouldn't even recognize the fruit.

84. Alcohol kills brain cells.

Alcohol makes new brain cells grow slower. Excessive drinking for years can cause interruptions when neurons are transferring information in your brain but it doesn't kill them.

85. Time makes beer go bad.

Light makes beer go bad, not time. That's why most beer is in green or brown bottles, not clear ones.

86. Sugar makes kids hyper.

Not one study has ever confirmed this. Sugar doesn't even make a difference when kids have ADHD.

87. No matter what your race, color, gender, sexuality, or religious beliefs are, we can all agree on one thing; airplane food sucks.

It's not the food that tastes bad. Even if you bring on your own food, it should taste mildly stale. This is because increased cabin pressure and low humidity, reduce your taste of salt and sweet food by a third.

88.　If you drop food, you can still eat it if you pick it up in less than five seconds.
　　Bacteria doesn't hang around for five seconds to "give you a chance to pick it up." The food is contaminated the second it touches the germ-infested floor.

89.　If you eat nine bananas in a row, you die from a potassium overdose.
　　Have you ever heard of anyone die this way?

90.　In the early nineties, a kid ate Pop Rocks and soda, which caused a chemical reaction that made his stomach explode, killing him.
　　This is one of the most famous urban legends ever. This rumor came about because Pop Rocks were falsely accused of having a huge amount of acid/base mixtures, which become explosive when mixed with fizzy drinks.
　　John Gilchrist, the person that "supposedly died" is still alive today.

91.　Food used to be a lot healthier in the old days.
　　Until 1966, food didn't even have food labels. So not only would you not know the level of

protein or fat in a food, but you couldn't even know if a food contained an ingredient that could cause a lethal allergic reaction.

I know the preservatives that are put into food and salt aren't healthy.

But do you know what's even less healthy? Rotting food. That's what you would be eating if your meat didn't have preservatives in it.

92. When toast falls butter-side down, it's because the universe hates you.

Seriously…why does it always land butter-side down. It's not 50/50. It's far more likely that it will land on the side you want to eat. What are the odds?

Very likely, actually. It's simple physics. If you drop toast, it's about three or four feet from the ground. This only gives it enough time to flip about 180 degrees. Since people eat toast with the butter facing you, if you dropped it, it will land with butter facing the ground.

93. Too much red meat gives you cancer.

Inuits eat almost nothing but red meat but they stay in great health. The Masai are an African tribe that eats mostly red meat and they rarely succumb to cancer or heart diseases.

Red meat isn't bad. Processed red meat is what's dangerous. To preserve meat, they are filled with additives and salts that are linked to many diseases.

Eating red meat is totally fine so long as it's unprocessed and fresh.

GAMES

94. The first modern Olympics Games was in Athens in Greece.
The first modern Olympics was anti-climatically in Shropshire in England.

95. An Olympic Gold Medal is made of gold.
At least 92.5% of all Gold Medals are made of silver. An extremely small amount is made of gold.

96. The first Olympics Games used the discus.
The original Olympics had only one event – running.

97. "Paralympics" is an abbreviation for "Paraplegic Olympics."
"Paralympics" is short for "Parallel Olympics."

98. If you are caught in a casino counting cards, you will have your winnings taken from you, you will be beaten up and thrown in jail for up to fifteen years.
Counting cards isn't illegal. If you are caught counting cards in a casino, you will be asked to leave (but you can keep your winnings.)

However, the casino will use facial recognition to memorize your face into a computer. They will use this technology not only to bar you from the casino but they will send it to other casinos so you will not be allowed to gamble anywhere.

99. Cheerleading is a fun sport.

Cheerleading causes more broken bones, paralyzing injuries, and even deaths than the ten most dangerous female sports. Combined.

What's more depressing is that cheerleading isn't technically a dangerous sport because it is not a classified sport. Cheerleaders have been fighting for years to be considered a sport but no such luck yet.

100. Ouija boards communicate with the dead.

You may be wondering what Ouija boards are doing in the "Games" section of my book. Ouija boards were made as a game by Elijah Bond in 1890. They were never intended to speak to the dead.

So why does the counter move then?

The counter moves through the ideomotor effect. If you tried to keep your hand completely still, it's impossible. Your hands will eventually move. If you are holding a counter, and someone says, "Left" over and over, your brain will unconsciously take it as a command. You might only move it less than a millimeter but after ten minutes of the same command, your hands can move the counter anywhere on the board.

The brand owners advertised it by saying your subconscious would guide you around the board to give yourself a message like your mood or your insecurities. But as the ideomotor effect shows, it's your unconscious mind being stimulated, not your subconscious.

101. The most well paid sportsman ever is Tiger Woods.

Although Tiger Woods is worth over a billion dollars, Diocles of Ancient Rome was worth far more.

Diocles was a charioteer who won almost 1,500 races and was rewarded the equivalent of $15 billion!

102. Football is a sport invented in England.

Football was a Chinese sport. The first known game was as early as 4 B.C. It was played almost identically to the way we know the game today.

103. Baseball originated in America.

Baseball came from England. It is not known exactly when but it is first described in a book called A Little Pretty Pocket Book that dates back to 1744.

104. Swimming less than an hour after eating will give your horrific cramps.

This was first published in Scouting for Boys in 1908. It was considered a potentially lethal danger.

It was dismissed in 1961 by exercise physiologist, Arthur Steinhaus and it hasn't been taken seriously since.

105. Ping-Pong is a game.

Originally, Ping-Pong was not the name of the game. The game was called whiff-whaff.

Ping-Pong was the name of a brand of whiff-whaffs. When the game was popularized, people assumed the brand name was the game's title.

This would be like seeing a runner with Nike shoes and thinking that all shoes were called Nikes, whether it was a boot, a wellie, or a clog.

HISTORY

106. Ninjas wore pure black.
The "ninja outfit" is a Kabuki costume. In Japanese theatre, Kabukis are stagehands. They would change the set in-between scenes. They would wear black outfit covering them from head-to-toe so the audience wouldn't see them to avoid "ruining the illusion of theatre." Kabuki translates into "we are not here." It was never used by ninjas.

This outfit is the WORST disguise ever (especially in the day time.) You would stick out like a kabuki in a crowd.

Ninjas looked like normal people, usually under the guise of an underling job like a farmer so they wouldn't stand out.

If a ninja had to commit a stealthy job at night, they would wear a stealth outfit.

But it was blue. We can see in the dark. It's not pitch black. Dark blue blends into the night better than black.

107. People jumped from skyscrapers during the Wall Street crash.
The comedian Will Rogers said this as a joke. A total of two people committed suicide by jumping out of buildings in the Wall Street crash of 1929. Neither of them were bankers.

108. Cowboys looked like cowboys.

The first cowboys were Mexican. They even made up a lot of the cowboy slang like "bronco," "stampede," and "lariat." This is why a three-man duel was called a Mexican standoff.

The hats never looked like "cowboy hats" at any point. They either looked like a flat hat, bowlers, or a slanted top hat.

Cowboys like Billy the Kid wore a shoddy top hat, not a cowboy hat.

109. The Wild West was wild.

The most people to ever be murdered during the Wild West era in a town was five.

I haven't seen Once Upon a Time in the West in a few years but I'll assume more people die in the first twenty minutes.

Even the legendary Billy the Kid only killed four people (in a top hat.)

Handguns weren't often used. Guns aren't fully reliable nowadays. Even a sophisticated gun can still get jammed. How often do you think that happened when they were still figuring how guns worked? They would've considered arm-wrestling before they considered a duel.

110. King Henry VIII was a fat king.

Many people find Henry VIII's depiction in the television show The Tudors a typical example of movie studios romanticizing history by making the king a handsome, well-built cuckold instead of a grossly obese monarch.

When he was a young king, King Henry VIII was known for being incredibly muscular and athletic. He took horse riding and sports very seriously. Sadly, this was his undoing. A horrific horse-riding accident left him in so much agony; he was practically bed-ridden for the last ten years of his life, which made him balloon up to 400 pounds.

111. King Henry VIII had six wives.

Henry himself said his first marriage "didn't count." His authority on this decision was accepted because he was the head of the Church of England.

Henry's second marriage was considered illegal according to the Pope because he was still married to his first wife. Henry's fourth and fifth marriage were annulled which means that they legally never happened. So only his third and sixth marriages are considered "real marriages."

112. Neanderthals looked like apes.

Neanderthals didn't hunch like an ape. They had great posture.

Nor did they have an ape-like face or excess body hair. Their facial structure was mildly different to our own. Their body was similar to us but stockier.

Neanderthals looked so human that if one wore modern clothes, you probably couldn't tell the difference.

113. Neanderthals grunted instead of speaking.

Scientists have found hyoid bones in Neanderthal remains. The hyoid bone is part of the vocal chords. After studying the hyoid, scientists said it was identical to how the human bones are structured so Neanderthals would be able to speak.

114. Neanderthals were our ancestors.

Neanderthals lived with our ancestors until the Neanderthals died out 30,000 years ago.

115. Neanderthals were stupid.

Neanderthals were at least as intelligent as us. It is debated that they were probably smarter. They were physically superior as well. They were stronger, taller, had better stamina, and handcrafted better tools.

So why did they die out? Ironically, Neanderthals died out because they were more mature than us. They reached full maturity at sixteen. So when our ancestors invaded their homes and attacked them, Neanderthals were too civilized to fight back. They were focusing on running away or protecting their families rather than killing. Sadly, this was their undoing.

116. Cavemen lived in caves.

Our Stone Age ancestors were excellent at building homes quickly and efficiently. Their homes were simple but sturdy and fitted their needs.

Living in caves was uncommon and tended to happen out of desperation like if there was a sudden change of weather or to hide from predators.

Some of our ancestors did live in caves long-term but many more people live in caves nowadays in poverty-stricken countries. China has 40 million cave dwellers today.

117. Those who were accused of witchcraft were burned at the stake.

You might think you are clever and think they were hung or drowned. But most women accused of being witches were acquitted.

During the Salem witch trials during Puritan times; if a person was accused of being a witch, they could avoid death by admitting to witchcraft or accusing someone else.

Some people refused to admit to witchcraft, worried that it would disgrace their family name. Those few were punished by being hung, not burned.

118. During the Bronze Age, people mostly used bronze.

In this time, nearly all people used stone. Bronze was extremely rare. It would be like calling modern times The AntiMatter Age. Antimatter exists, but you're never going to see it in your entire life.

The "Bronze" Age was between 2,300 – 600 BC. Bronze became common in 1,200 BC- 400 AD... which is confusing because this was right smack in the middle of the Iron Age (where people actually used iron.)

119. The Ice Age ended 10,000 years ago.

The last Ice Age hasn't ended yet. People worry that global warming may cause another Ice Age not realizing that we are in one.

By definition, an Ice Age ends when the polar ice caps melt. The next full-blown Ice Age isn't expected to happen for 12,000 years.

120. A barbarian is a wild savage.

"Barbarian" was a word used by the Ancient Greeks to describe anyone who wasn't Greek.

They claimed that non-Greeks all sounded the same and made noises like, "Bar-bar-bar-bar."

121. Ancient Greek statues looked the same as they do now.

All marble statues (and many buildings and structures) were extremely colorful in Ancient Greece. All of the purple, red, blue, green, and yellow have faded due to rain and time. In their day, everything looked like a hallucinogenic disco.

122. Chastity belts existed.

Chastity belts are a fictional concoction having no place in history.

There are some to this day which can be seen in museums that are completely fake.

A chastity belt would be pretty impractical if you needed to use the toilet.

123. "Saved by the bell" is a phrase that came from the idea that people were buried alive in Victorian times.

People were so scared of being buried alive that they had strings in coffins attached to a bell above ground. If a person woke up in a coffin, buried alive, they would tug the string, the bell would ring and people above would dig them out. This means they were "saved by the bell."

This was said to inspire Dracula. The bell idea was seriously considered but there isn't a single example of someone ever being "saved by the bell."

But that's not where that expression comes from. It was originally used in boxing when the bell rang just before a boxer was about to be knocked out.

124. Neil Armstrong's flag is still on the Moon.

Most people believe the America flag is still on the Moon.

However, it was too near Armstrong's lunar module, and when the ship lifted off, the flag was blown away.

125. The Bubonic Plague originated in Europe.

The Black Death originated in Europe but the Bubonic Plague has been around for millennia (and it's still around today.)

The earliest record of this plague was in China 2,600 years ago.

126. Selfies are a recent fad.

If you hate the "selfies" fad, guess what? Selfies existed shortly after the camera was invented. There are pictures of selfies that date back to 1839. I don't know if this is reassuring or more depressing.

127. In the last generation, teachers could legally beat disobedient children.

You may have heard your parents or grandparents say, "You think school is tough? In my day, teachers would whack us with a cane if we misbehaved!"

Sadly, flogging students still occurs today. In nineteen states in America, a teacher can hit a child with a wooden paddle for talking out of turn or if their shirt is untucked. In 2012, nearly 40,000 children were flogged just in Mississippi.

128. Rap battles have been around for a few decades.

Norse Vikings challenged each other to rap battles as early as the fifth century. Two people would take turns churning out insults in verse. It was called flyting but it was the same format as has been seen in Eminem's movie, 8 Mile.

129. Yoga is thousands of years old.

Yoga goes as far back as....1960. So your grandparents were around before yoga.

You may doubt this because you have seen old pictures of people in the yoga stance. That stance is how most people sit on a flat surface. They are not doing yoga. They are sitting down on the floor. If you were so poor, you couldn't afford furniture, where else could you sit?

THE HUMAN BODY

130. **The funny bone is a bone.**
The reason why the funny bone hurts so much when it gets hit is because that pain is not from a bone but a nerve called the ulnar nerve. It's called the "funny bone" because it's near the humerus bone.

131. **Blood clots are caused on planes by decompressed air.**
Decompressed air can't lead to blood clots alone.

You may think it has to do with sitting still for a long period of time. But you have sat still for hours at school or when you watched tv. Decompressed air or sitting still are not harmful by themselves. It's the combination of the two that can be potentially lethal.

132. **If you are about to have a heart attack, you will have a sharp paralyzing pain in your left arm and chest.**
A lot of heart attacks give no warning. Half of the people who have heart attacks suffer silently. This gives you less time to get to a doctor and these types of heart attacks are considered more lethal. The type of pain can vary. You might feel

dizzy, paranoid, panicky, or feel an intense toothache.

133. **The strongest muscle is the bicep.**
The strongest muscle in the human body is the tongue.

Although your biceps are strong, they need to pull other muscles to work. The tongue is the only muscle to be attached only by one end. As a result, it heavily relies on its own strength.

134. **If there is a hostage situation with an armed man, snipers try to shoot the assailant in the head.**
Snipers try to shoot the assailant in the top lip. Behind the top lip is the part of the brain that controls reflexes. Shooting someone here will prevent the assailant firing his or her gun on reflex.

135. **If you play classical music to a pregnant woman daily, her unborn child will grow up to be super intelligent.**
This myth is called the Mozart Effect. Listening to classical music may relax a woman when she's pregnant which will be calming for the unborn child but it won't boost the fetus' intelligence.

136. The large intestine is larger than the smaller intestine.
    The large intestine looks bigger because it surrounds the small intestine but if you spread them out, the small intestine would be twenty feet while the large intestine would be five feet.

137. Drugs can create holes in your brain.
    Excessive drug addiction can cause irreversible affects to your mind but it can't create a hole in your brain.

138. Humans are born as a blank slate.
    Depending on the pregnant woman's mood, diet, and genetics, the fetus will develop characteristics which can be set in stone before it is even born.

139. If you have a high IQ, you're super smart.
    To quote Stephen Hawking, who's probably the smartest person alive, "I have no idea what my IQ is. People who boast about their IQ are losers."
    IQ tests can help you understand certain strengths and weaknesses like spatial awareness and assess three-dimensional patterns. When we think of intelligence, most people think of academic intelligence. But what about experiential, creative, practical, contextual,

componential, analytical, interpersonal, verbal-linguistic, logical-mathematical, intrapersonal, musical, emotional, or social intelligence? There is no single test you can do that encapsulates your overall intelligence. Whatever you're good at, you will always be bad at something else. People will always tend to balance out and having a supposedly high IQ shouldn't signify anything about your ability or your intelligence over anybody else.

140. Your voice sounds the way you hear it.

Your mouth and ears are close to each other so when you speak, your ears hear your voice differently than how everybody else hears it.

Let's do an experiment - Put your hands in-between your ears and your cheekbones with your thumbs sticking outward. If you speak now, you will hear yourself the way other people do.

141. You look the way you see yourself in the mirror.

Did you ever look at a photo of yourself with a group of friends and wonder why you look weird? It's not the camera. Everybody else looks normal.

There's something wrong with your face but you can't place it.

The reason why people tend to not like themselves in photographs is because they are used to seeing their reversed image in a mirror. You see your left features on your right and vice versa. Pictures show you for how you really look but it jars with your brain because it is used to seeing a reversed image. A photograph is how everyone sees you and a mirror is just how you see yourself.

142. If you covered someone in gold paint from head to toe, they would die from suffocation.

This idea has become popular thanks to the movie, Goldfinger. There has been an archaic theory that we breathe through our skin as well as our mouth and nose. This idea is unfounded. I wouldn't recommend being covered in gold paint, but you can obviously breathe through your nose and mouth.

143. Television damages your eyes.

Early televisions use to emit a low level of radiation so people were advised not to sit too near it. This hasn't been a concern for fifty years.

Too much tv is bad for you because it creates a lazy and addictive lifestyle but it doesn't damage your eyesight.

144. Reading in dim light damages your eyesight.

In dim light, the muscles around the pupils contract so they can let in more light. It can strain your eyes but it won't impair them in the long run.

145. Watching television doesn't burn calories.

We burn more calories when we are scared because our heart is racing which means blood is pumped faster around our body.

So if you want to lose a few pounds, try giving The Exorcist a watch.

146. You can test if someone has taken drugs by examining their urine.

In this day and age, urine tests are still not foolproof. Food, allergy medication, medicine for a cold or flu, antidepressants, and antibiotics can trigger a positive result in a drug test.

Sadly it works both ways. There are many drugs that don't come across as a positive in a drug test. Lance Armstrong got away with it for over a decade.

147. Some people don't dream.

Everyone dreams every night. Some people don't remember their dreams. The average person has about nine dreams each night. Even a person who thinks they never dream has at least three or four dreams per night.

Your mind starts forgetting the dream seconds after you wake up and most dreams are completely lost within less than ten minutes.

148. If you are cold, you will catch a cold.

If you are cold, you will catch pneumonia before you catch a cold. A cold is a virus. You catch it from people. This is common in cold weather because you spend more time inside with other people to catch it from.

149. Latinos and black people can't have blonde or ginger hair.

Sofia Vergara is a Latino actress with natural blonde hair who regularly gets asked by casting directors why she dyed her hair blonde.

Latino's can have red or blonde hair. It is just rarer in their genes.

The same applies to black people. Both parents need to have a certain gene for their child to be red-headed or blonde but it's not impossible.

Melanesian people of New guinea and some Pacific islands have black people with blond, curly hair.

150. You should clean your ears with cotton buds.

Earwax naturally cleans your ears. Pushing a cotton bud into your ear will push the earwax further down your ear making you far more prone to infections. Your ears are self-cleaning. It's okay to use a cotton bud a couple of times a year but doctors would strongly recommend you don't use them routinely.

151. Brain cells can't regenerate.

This can't be true. New cells will replace every cell in your body within nine years. Some of your cells last days. Some cells last years. Within nine years, brand new cells, including in your brain, will have replaced every single cell in your body.

152. If you fall from a great height and land in water, you should be fine.

A person falling sixty meters would be falling at 120mph. 80mph would be fatal so hitting water at 120mph would have the same effect on your body as landing on concrete.

153. You need to wash your hair every day.

I did that. I went bald at 22. That kind of backfired.

Your hair produces natural oils that will preserve your hair for longer. Shampooing it everyday doesn't allow your hair a chance to do this.

154. Your hair and nails grow for three days after death.

When you die, your body becomes completely dehydrated which causes your skin to shrink back making your nails and hair look longer.

No cells can grow without a source of glucose, which stops being produced after death.

155. The more you shave, the thicker the hair grows back.

If that were true, I would still have hair.

156. You are allergic to _____.

Few people have genuine allergies.

You may think, "But I can't eat wheat or pasta or citric acid, etc."

Those are intolerances. Intolerances have mild side effects e.g. bloating, headaches, rash, drowsiness, ulcers, and so on.

An allergy is dangerous reaction. An allergy to medication or peanuts can cause paralysis, brain damage, impotence, or death.

157. You can't tickle yourself.
   You can tickle yourself in one spot – the roof of your mouth.

158. When you are old, you have fewer brain cells than when you were in your prime.
   Society thinks that only 50% of your brain cells are functioning when you get to your seventies.
   A person in their seventies has 97% the brain cells they had when they were twenty.

159. The dirtiest part of the human body is the underwear area.
   This is the cleanest area because it's tightly sealed twofold by trousers and underwear.
   The dirtiest parts of your body are the most exposed body parts – your hands. Your face gets a lot of bacteria and germs too but your hands are especially prone to this because they are touching surfaces, opening doors, etc.

160. You should wash your hands after you use the toilet.
   Now that you know the hands are the dirtiest part of the human body, you will understand that the most logical time to wash your hands is BEFORE you use the toilet.

161. It takes more muscles to frown than to smile.

There are fifty-three facial muscles. It takes twelve to smile. It takes eleven to frown.

Look at it this way, if you smile, you burn slightly more calories.

162. Your nerves are hundreds of feet long.

If you stretched your nerves out, they would reach nearly forty-five miles.

That's a lot of nerve.

163. Testosterone makes people aggressive.

A lack of testosterone makes people aggressive.

The reason why is not understood but many tests have been done by countless researches and it always results in the same thing; people act friendlier when given testosterone.

People only get aggressive when they are TOLD they have been given testosterone (even if they received a placebo.)

164. When you are hot, drink a cold drink to cool down and vice versa.

External heat will affect your body temperature, but not as much as internal heat. If you drink a cold soda when you are too hot, your body temperature will react to the cold drink by making you feel warmer. So attempting to stay cool will make you hotter.

When hot, drink hot drinks. When cold, drink cold drinks.

INVENTIONS

165. **Leonardo Da Vinci invented the helicopter.**

Da Vinci famously drew sketches of guns, tanks, submarines, and helicopters long before they were invented.

The helicopter gets special credit because if it were built according to his designs, it would've actually worked. Or so they say.

Not only is this not true, but the Chinese invented a helicopter in the fourth century. It was a small toy called a bamboo dragon.

People may debate this because it was only a few inches tall. Skeptics would say a "real helicopter" is one that can fit a person in it.

That's not the definition. A helicopter is simply a device that can hover with a rapid moving propeller.

166. **Da Vinci invented the parachute.**

4,000 years ago, a Chinese emperor called Shun ran from his murderous father by climbing to the top of a building. With nowhere to go, he grabbed a bunch of bamboo hats, leapt off the building, and glided downward to safety. It's very basic but it is the first record of a parachute.

167. The cuckoo clock comes from Switzerland.

Orson Welles said this "fact" in one of the most famous monologues in movie history in the film The Third Man.

Fantastic movie. Totally not true though. It was invented in Germany.

168. E-readers like Kindles are a recent invention.

A teacher called Angela Ruiz invented the e-reader in 1949. She came up with the idea to stop her pupils from carrying heavy books.

Her creation was surprisingly advanced. In her version, the reader could zoom in on sections and the screen lit up so it could be read at night. This sounds basic now, but this was back in the 40s when it was uncommon to afford a tv.

Sadly, she could never find the funding to make one single prototype.

169. Touchscreen is a recent invention.

Touchscreens were implemented in Switzerland in CERN's laboratories twenty years ago. They were too clunky so touchscreen didn't catch on until the much-easier-to-use smartphones.

170. Smartphones are a recent invention.
The first smartphone was in 1994 by IBM.
You may assume it was very rudimentary but it could send emails, had predictive text and had some basic apps.
You might think it was a commercial failure but IBM still get royalties from it today and make billions from the smartphone market.

171. Ice skates were invented in the last few hundred years.
The Finnish made ice skates out of bones 5,000 years ago. They relied on them to travel vast distances and conserve heat and energy in freezing weather.

172. Galileo invented the telescope.
Hans Lippershey invented the telescope in 1608. Galileo heard of the invention and made a drastically better version a few years later.

173. The CIA invented house arrest tracers.
No, and it wasn't the FBI, NSA, or the police. It was Spiderman.
I don't mean a guy called Bill Spiderman. I mean the superhero Spiderman.
In the comics in 1979, a villain called the Kingpin placed a tracer on Spiderman so he would always know where Spiderman was.

At the same time, Judge Jack Love (I thought only comic-book characters had names like that) realized that prisons were becoming overcrowded.

He happened to read this comic and came up with the idea of house-arresting criminals with tracers to prevent overfilling prisons.

174. Batteries were invented in the last two centuries.

Batteries have been found that date back to 200 B.C.

The first battery is known as the Baghdad Battery. It is not known what it was used for but it has all the makings of a battery – rod, cylinder, electrolyte, and negative terminal.

LAW

175. Slavery is at an all time low in the world.
Despite slavery being illegal in every country, slavery worldwide is at an all time high. There are 27 million slaves in the world. That's more than every African shipped to the New World in the history of the Trans-Atlantic slave trade.

China has the most with nearly three million. Even America has 50,000 slaves.

176. The US Constitution has the phrase, "Life, Liberty, and the Pursuit of Happiness."
That is the Declaration of Independence.
Now let's see what else is not mentioned in the American Constitution.

177. The Constitution mentions God.
Not once.

178. The Constitution mentions Democracy.
Nah.

179. The Constitution says, "Everyone is innocent until proven guilty."
Not even a little bit.

180. The Constitution says, "Marriage is between a man and a woman."

This was one of the central arguments when the laws were changed recently to allow same-sex marriages. Bigots would cry out, "It's in the Constitution!"

But as you should have guessed, it isn't.

181. The Constitution stipulates, "Everyone has the right to vote."

This is not mentioned anywhere (which is a big deal because that means the government can deny any voter if they choose to.)

182. You get one phone call after you get arrested.

This was invented for television. Standard cells should be equipped with a phone. You can make as many calls as you want so long as they are prepaid or collect calls. The phones are only usable at specific times (normally 6am-10pm.) You can lose your call rights if you misbehave.

183. A criminal can plead insanity to be sent to a psychiatric ward to avoid jail.

This tactic is rarely tried and almost never works. Being in a psychiatric ward can be more terrifying than prison. Three US states have completely banned the insanity defense.

184. Using fingerprints to identify criminals has been practiced for about a century.
   This practice is over 4,000 years old and originated in Babylon.

185. Prohibition made it illegal to drink alcohol.
   During Prohibition, alcohol could be consumed but it couldn't be transported or sold.

186. You need to wait 24 hours before filing a missing person's report.
   This is often used as a plot device to build tension in a movie but it's untrue. You can file a report after any time if there is sufficient evidence a person is missing.

187. If a cop doesn't say the Miranda Rights (You have the right to remain silent, etc.) while arresting someone, the person being arrested can't go to jail.
   The film, 21 Jump Street, has popularized this idea. I'm pretty sure that if a person shot a cop at point blank range in front of fifty witnesses and was on live television AND admitted he did it, Miranda Rights or not, that guy is going to jail.

MISCELLANEOUS

188. Pencils have lead.
There has never been lead in pencils. Pencils are made of graphite.

189. If there's an earthquake, stand in a doorway.
A doorway will make no difference when a powerful earthquake demolishes your house. Your best bet is to hide under a table.

190. Suicide is highest during the holidays.
Statistically in most countries (especially America) the most common time of the year for suicide is April or May.

191. A lit cigarette can ignite a gasoline trail.
This looks cool in movies but a cigarette doesn't give out enough heat to light gasoline.

192. People can fit in ventilation shafts.
This has been seen in countless films. A human being couldn't fit in most ventilation shafts. Even if they could, they are not designed to support a person's weight.

193. Owning 51% of the shares in a company means you own the company.

As you can see by the previous two facts and this one, a lot of misconceptions come entirely from movies. There is a common plot device in movies where a guy buys 51% of a company and then fires the boss and nobody can legally stop him.

A majority in a stock-based company can outvote any individual, even if they hold 51% of stock or more.

194. Skydivers pull a cord to make their parachute pop open.

Cords haven't been used in twenty years. Skydivers release a pin instead. Pulling a cord looks cooler in movies so modern films still use them.

195. Skydivers can hear each other.

No matter how loud you yell, you won't be able to hear anything anyone says as you plummet down to Earth at 100mph.

196. When skydivers deploy their chute, they shoot back up.

Skydivers can't go back up. When you see a skydiver in a video clip or a movie, they look like they are shooting up when they deploy their chute because the cameraman is still falling at 100mph while the skydiver is slowing down dramatically.

197. Mental institutions use straitjackets.

By law, institutions have to use the least restrictive restraints possible. Patients lashing out will be sedated with medication.

198. When lightning strikes, hide under a tree.

Trees can explode when struck by lightning, making the bark shred your body like shrapnel. The most intelligent place to hide during a lightning strike is inside a car.

MOVIES

199. Sean Connery has hair in the James Bond movies.

Connery went bald when he was 22. He is wearing a toupee in every Bond film. You can even see him adjusting it in the DVD extras.

200. In the James Bond movies, Q's real name is undisclosed.

Desmond Llewelyn played Q in the James Bond movies for forty-six years. But in Desmond's first performance in From Russia With Love, he is called by his surname, which is Boothroyd.

It is mentioned in the novels that his first name is Geoffrey.

201. The ending of Blade Runner is ambiguous.

Blade Runner is based off Philip K. Dick's book, Do Robots Dream of Electric Sheep? In the book, the main character, Deckard is not a Replicant (an android who believes he is human.)

The movie's director Ridley Scott said that Deckard (played by Harrison Ford) is definitely a Replicant. His Director's Cut makes this far clearer than the original version.

202. The ending of Total Recall is ambiguous.

This 1990 movie is also based on a book by Philip K. Dick book (what's with this guy and ambiguous endings that aren't actually ambiguous?)

In the movie, the main character Quaid doesn't know who he is. He is either a secret agent or a brain-damaged comatose patient having a dream.

The movie ends by fading to white. Usually, movies fade to black. It is said that people see a bright light before they die. This white light is meant to symbolize that Quaid's dream has ended and he has died in his coma.

This is not ambiguous. This has been completely confirmed by the director Paul Verhoeven.

203. Ewoks are mentioned in Star Wars.

"Ewok" isn't said once at any point in any of the movies.

204. No one knows what Bill Murray says to Scarlett Johansson at the end of Lost in Translation.

I do.

If you're a big fan of this movie, don't read this. People have debated this for over a decade and the answer will ruin the ambiguity.

There's no way to hear it all but you can barely hear Murray say, "When John is waiting on the next business trip…. Go up to that man, and tell him the truth. Okay?"

I'll assume whatever you imagined he said was more interesting than that.

205. Fargo is based on a true story.

I know the tag line is "Based on a true story" but everyone who worked on the movie knew it was fictional.

206. The Texas Chainsaw Massacre is based on a true story.

The movie's killer, "Leatherface" is inspired by real life serial killer Ed Gein. But the circumstances of the film never happened. Gein also inspired the killer in Psycho and Silence of the Lambs.

207. No one knows what was in the briefcase in Pulp Fiction.

It was diamonds.

The director's last movie, Reservoir Dogs revolved around diamonds. He didn't want to do another "diamonds movie" so they are never seen on camera and nobody references them as "diamonds."

208. In Pulp Fiction, Jules reads a quote from the Bible called Ezekiel 25:17.

The only part that is even close to Ezekiel 25:17 is,

"I will execute great vengeance on them with wrathful punishments. Then they shall know that I am the Lord, when I lay my vengeance on them."

The rest is the script taking artistic liberties.

MUSIC

209. The Sydney Opera House is the best opera house in the world.
The Sydney Opera House is the biggest and most famous opera house but it is considered to have the worst acoustics of all the major opera houses worldwide because it is too big.

It will realistically get shut down in the near future.

210. Violin strings are made of catgut.
Catgut isn't from a cat. When catgut is used (which is rare,) it normally comes from a goat but it can be a pig or donkey.

Nowadays, most violin strings are made from steel or synthetic material.

211. "Every Breath You Take" by the Police is a romantic song.
This song is not remotely romantic. It's about a stalker in the process of stalking. Listen to the lyrics and tell me if they sound sweet or disturbing.

"Every step you take, every move you make, I'll be watching you."

That's why the band is called The Police. Because that's who you call if a person ever plays this song to you.

212. "Lucy in the Sky with Diamonds" by the Beatles is an allegory to drugs.

John Lennon's son Julian drew a picture of his friend Lucy in playgroup looking at the sky and surrounded it with diamonds.

John was inspired to write a song about something his son loved.

He did not realize until later that the title's initials are LSD.

213. "Puff the Magic Dragon" by the Beatles is an allegory to drugs.

The Beatles sang it but it was written by Peter Yarrow who said he was, "too square to write about something like that."

214. Jeff Buckley wrote the song, "Hallelujah."

His version is the most famous but Leonard Cohen wrote it.

215. Michael Jackson invented the moonwalk.

A musician called Bill Bailey invented the dance in 1955.

216. Michael Jackson had surgery to make him white.

Michael Jackson claimed to have a pigmentation disorder called vitiligo. He claimed that his skin color was patchy and he bleached his skin to even it out. This wasn't widely believed but his autopsy has confirmed that Jackson definitely had vitiligo.

217. Michael Jackson had hair.

During a Pepsi commercial, a pyrotechnic malfunction burned Jackson's hair. He had to wear a wig to his dying day.

218. Bob Marley sang the song, "Don't Worry, Be Happy."

I've heard this song many times sang over images of Bob Marley.

It was sang by Bob McFerrin years after Marley died.

PEOPLE

219. Pocahontas' name was Pocahontas.
Her name was Matoaka. Pocahontas is the name her tribe gave her when she went with the Settlers. It translates into "frisky" but it was considered incredibly insulting.

220. Napoleon Bonaparte was short.
The French measuring system at the time said Napoleon was 5ft 2. Using conventional measuring units, Napoleon was 5ft 7, which was slightly above average at the time.

221. Martin Luther King wrote the speech, "I Had a Dream."
On that day, the crowd received pamphlets with King's prepared speech. He didn't feel like reading it. Instead, he made up his own speech and spontaneously improvised his "I Had a Dream" monologue on the spot and created one of the greatest speeches of all time.

222. Martin Luther King was incredibly popular at the time of this death.
King was against the Vietnam War, which made him lose supporters. Documentary maker Michael Moore said when he was a kid, he came

out of a church when the news confirmed King was dead. People cheered and applauded.

223. Quakers invented Quaker Oats.
Henry Parsons Crowell bought the bankrupt Quaker Oat Mill Company and trademarked the name. He himself was not a Quaker.

224. Richard III was hunched, had a clubbed foot, a deformed hand and a disfigured face.
Ok...exaggerating imperfections in powerful people is common. Satirical drawings always give Nixon a big nose.

This image people have of Richard III is a smear campaign on steroids.

Richard's skeleton was unearthed recently. It showed none of these physical deformities.

225. Gandhi's first name was Mahatma.
Mahatma was his title. It means "great soul." His name was Mohandas.

226. The most recognizable character in the world is Jesus Christ.
Jesus may look easily identifiable to you but that's only if you are from the Western world.

Could you distinguish the differences between Krishna, Vishnu, and Kali?

A person from the Western world may not be able to tell the subtle but distinctive differences between Krishna and Vishnu just like someone from the East may not be able to distinguish Jesus Christ from any other Biblical figure.

Some would argue the most recognizable figure, fictitious or otherwise, would be Superman or Batman.

This is logical because they are popular superheroes. But they have same problem as Christ (Yes, I am suggesting Batman has the same problems as Jesus.) To people in the Eastern world that are unfamiliar with comics, they couldn't distinguish one guy in tights with a cape to another guy in tights with a cape.

But the most recognizable character in the world IS a superhero.

The massive, green, muscular superhero, the Incredible Hulk has such a distinctive appearance, that he is the world's most recognized character.

227. TMZ are the worst journalists ever.

TMZ are arguably the most reliable source of information on the Internet. I kid you not. More so than IMDB, Wikipedia, Cracked, or that Dolphin guy on Reddit who somehow knows everything.

They get a bad reputation because they invade the private lives of celebrities and seem desperate for gossip. But what have they said that isn't true?

They seem irritating because TMZ is mentioned when there's an incident in Hollywood but that's because they tend to be the first to confirm a lot of news. They were the first to confirm that Paul Walker and Michael Jackson were dead.

228. Saint Nicholas who inspired Santa Claus was from Lapland.

St. Nick was from Turkey.

229. Sigmund Freud was the father of modern psychology.

Pierre Janet first theorized psychoanalysis, hysteria, dissociation, and having a relationship with a patient.

His rival, Freud published Janet's theories as his own and walked away with all of the credit.

230. Sigmund Freud is from Germany.

No, and it's not Austria either.

Sigmund Freud was from Moravia, which no longer exists. It has been absorbed by Czech Republic.

231. St. Patrick was Irish.
St. Patrick (or to use his real name, Maewyn Succat) was either Welsh or Scottish. He was kidnapped and shipped to Ireland at sixteen as a slave.

When he became a priest years later, he took the name Patrick to honor Saint Patricius.

232. Muhammed Ali defeated Sonny Lipton in the legendary "Phantom Punch Fight."
This is now a classic poster with the caption– First Round. First Minute.

This picture helped define Muhammed Ali as a champion and a legend.

But it's against the rules not to return to your corner after a knockdown. Lipton should have continued but the referee unfairly ruled a knock out.

233. Elvis Presley had jet-black hair.
Elvis dyed his hair black for most of his career. He was blond.

234. King Edward "Longshanks" was an evil tyrant during the time of William Wallace.
Longshanks was invited by Scotland at this time to help the Scottish people.

He is responsible for creating dozens of laws and formed the first constitution in England.

He would be considered one of the best kings of his time.

235. The Mayan civilization is extinct.

Seven million Mayans are alive today, mainly in Mexico and Guatemala. In case you're wondering, no, they are not savages. Many of them are completely assimilated into modern society.

236. Isaac Newton had an epiphany about gravity when an apple fell on his head from a tree.

Newton never references this in his writings. It was probably mentioned by the writer, Voltaire first and intended to be a joke.

237. Michelangelo painted the Sistine Chapel lying on his back on a platform.

This idea came from the 1965 movie, The Agony and the Ecstasy where Charlton Heston played Michelangelo. In reality, Michelangelo was on a platform but he painted the ceiling standing, the same way as any painter. It gave him incredible strain on his neck.

In the movie, they probably did it with Heston lying on his back to avoid him being injured in a similar fashion.

238. Pope Joan was a secret female pope that got found out when she gave birth to a child.

That would make a great movie but it's entirely fiction.

239. Captain Cook discovered Australia.

An English pirate called William Dampier and two Dutchmen called Abel Tasman and Dirk Hartog found Australia before Cook.

240. The western outlaw, Buffalo Bill killed buffalos.

Buffalos didn't exist in North America in Bill's time. He killed bison.

241. Houdini was the greatest magician ever.

Houdini was a great magician but he was a terrible showman. Houdini's original passion was acting but critics described him as being "wooden." This was a time when audiences were blown away by awful makeup and cardboard sets so Houdini must've been REALLY bad at acting.

Houdini would do one trick, and then move onto another trick and so on and so on. He didn't dress up his magic. He was so good that he indirectly made other amateur magicians create all of the gimmicks that we associate with magic like the presentation, build-up, beautiful assistants, dramatic lights, and music.

So why is he so famous? When Houdini realized he was considered boring and dull, he focused on escaping death-defying tricks and became known as the greatest escape artist of all time.

Houdini was known more as an escape artist than a magician back in his day.

242. Houdini died because somebody punched him in the stomach in the middle of a magic trick.

Houdini could tense his muscles so he could withstand a punch to the stomach. Supposedly, a muscular man asked him if he could punch Houdini in the stomach. Houdini agreed and before he had a chance to tense his muscles, the man punched Houdini in the gut full force several times. This was said to have burst Houdini's appendix, killing him shortly after.

Houdini did die from appendicitis but the story of the man punching him is not true. On Houdini's final tour, he complained of tummy pains but continued his tour. His appendix ruptured the same day as his final performance. He died several hours later.

243. Caligula was insane.

There are many insane "facts" about the Ancient Roman emperor Caligula. Caligula was said to order his men to fight the sea with swords to kill Neptune, the God of the Sea.

But he wasn't insane. There are several detailed biographies of him and each of them describes him as arrogant and aggressive. Only one biography has described him as a lunatic and it didn't come from a reliable source but people believed it because it was more interesting.

PLACES

244. There are fifty states in America.
There are forty-six states in America. The other four "states" Kentucky, Massachusetts, Pennsylvania, and Virginia are Commonwealths. They titled themselves as Commonwealths after the War of Independence and have never been reverted back to States.

245. Americans are getting dumber.
Graduation in high school and college are the highest they have been in America in forty years.

246. Americans are getting fatter.
Obesity in children has decreased 43% in children over the last ten years and overall obesity has leveled out for the first time in thirty years.

247. Gun related homicide in America is increasing.
Gun homicide was at its peak in America in 1993. It's down by 49% now.

248. Gun ownership is increasing in America.
One in three Americans have a gun compared to one in two Americans in the 1970s.

249. 10% of Americans have a passport.
America has the third highest international flight departures annually. 37% of Americans have a passport (approximately 120 million people.)

250. Cocaine and heroin are the most common drugs in America to overdose on.
More Americans overdose on prescription painkillers than heroin and cocaine combined.

251. The country that has the most cosmetic surgery is America.
South Korea has the record with 7.5 million of its inhabitants having cosmetic surgery.

252. Japan creates more soy sauce than any other country.
The Netherlands exports more soy sauce than even Japan.

253. Hiroshima and Nagasaki are uninhabitable because of radioactive fallout.
These two cities have been completely rebuilt. I have friends in Nagasaki. People get these cities mixed up with Chernobyl, which is uninhabitable for the next 10,000 years.

254. Africa is poor.
   Many parts of Africa are enriched with fertile land, oil, minerals, cars, electronics, fresh water, resources, and electricity.

255. Most of Africa is wilderness.
   28% of Africa is wilderness.
   38% of North America is wilderness.

256. The piñata comes from Mexico.
   The piñata was originally Chinese.

257. Ayers Rock in Australia is the world's biggest rock.
   Ayers Rock isn't even the biggest rock in Australia.
   The world's biggest rock is Mount Augustus. It's 858m high and five miles long. It's nearly two and a half times the size of Ayers Rock.
   It is located in Australia but for some reason Ayers Rock gets the reputation of Australia's most famous natural landmark.

258. Everyone in China is only allowed one child in order to control overpopulation and if they have any more, the child is killed.
   The one-child rule applies to only 35% of the population. It is an understandable rule if your

nation's population is over a billion, making up 13% of the world population.

If a parent is not taking precautions after having children, the government takes that seriously and the parents can be fined or arrested.

259. South Africa has the highest production of diamonds.

Russia has the highest worldwide production of diamonds at 22.4%. South Africa is fifth at 9%.

260. Switzerland has no guns.

People assume Switzerland doesn't have guns because it is famously considered "the neutral country" staying out of all wars.

Gun laws are extremely strict and highly regulated in Switzerland but almost every household must have a gun by law.

People in Switzerland have more guns per person than in Iraq.

RELIGION

261. Buddhism is common in India.
Less than 1% of Indians are Buddhists. There are far more Christians than Buddhists in India. Buddhism hasn't been a common religion in India for over a millennium. The most common religion in India by far is Hinduism.

262. Buddhists believe in reincarnation.
Reincarnation is a Hindu belief. When Buddhists talk about being reborn, they mean you can change as a person for the better. It doesn't convey a literal change into another person or creature.

263. Buddhists are pacifists.
In extreme situations, Buddhists will become violent to protect their loved ones, like any person would. They are not beyond defending themselves.

264. Buddhists meditate.
Not all Buddhists meditate in a yoga stance while chanting or humming. They can find other ways to find peace like music, walking, or exercise.

265. Buddhists worship their god Buddha.
Many Buddhists don't see Buddhism as a religion, but as a philosophy. Being at peace with oneself and meditating doesn't necessarily mean Buddhists need to have a relationship with God.

Buddha was not a God. He was a man. And there's one more thing people always get wrong about Buddha...

266. Buddha is a big, smiling, bald, fat man.
That fat, smiling statue you see everywhere is not Buddha.

Buddha (who's real name was Siddhartha Gautama) looked like a human skeleton. He rarely ate as he felt like he didn't need to eat to be happy. He only ate for sustenance.

That fat statue was a monk called Budai. It is not known for certain how he gets mixed up with Buddha. Some people have suggested that Westerners see happiness as "being big and jolly" so when they see this fat, smiling statue representing enlightenment and happiness, they assume he's Buddha.

267. Nearly all South Koreans are Buddhists.
22% of South Koreas are Buddhists, 29% are Christians, and 46% are atheists.

268. The Star of David is a Jewish symbol.
   The Star of David was a symbol in Buddhism, Hinduism, and Jainism before the Jews popularized it.

269. A.D. has always stood for Anno Domini, which is Latin for "In the Year of Our Lord."
   Ancient Roman emperor Diocleatius coined A.D. in his name. It stood for Anno Diocletian. Diocletius has been nearly forgotten now and as his influence faded, A.D. changed its meaning. When 247 A.D. ended in Diocleatius' name, the following year was 532 Anno Domini, 500 years after Christ's death.

270. If enough people put their religion as "Jedi" on a consensus form, a country would have to recognize it as an actual religion.
   Funny but untrue…sadly.
   Someday…someday…

271. Jesus Christ is white and looks like how he is presented in paintings in the Sistine Chapel and Da Vinci's The Last Supper.
   Since Jesus was from the Middle East, he would have a dark complexion. Jesus had short hair, as was custom with Jewish men at the time. It even says in Corinthians 11:14, "Doth not even

nature itself teach you that if a man have long hair it is a shame onto him?"

Despite what paintings would tell you, Jesus did not look like a Calvin Klein model. Isaiah 53:2b said that Jesus "had no beauty or majesty to attract us to Him, nothing in His appearance that we should desire Him." Many times, his apostles didn't even notice him in a room because he looked completely ordinary.

272. We were created in God's image.

This is a mistranslation. Making God look human in art is misinterpreting what "in God's image" means. It's referenced in Gen 1:27. The original wording "tselem demuth" means "having God-like attributes." This may be a reference how in the Bible, the first generations of mankind had greater longevity. Noah and Methuselah lived for over 900 years.

273. The Gospels of the Bible were written originally in Latin.

They were not written in Latin nor were they written in Hebrew. They weren't even written in Aramaic, the language Christ spoke. They were written in Greek (hence all of the mistranslations and misunderstandings.)

274. The Rapture is mentioned in the Bible.
The Rapture is the idea that the world will end when the Four Horsemen of the Apocalypse known as War, Pestilence, Famine, and Death walk the Earth destroying and killing everything.

The non-sinners ascend into heaven and the sinners are left behind to bear witness to the end of the world before they are cast down to Hell.

The Rapture wasn't a popular idea until the sixteenth century.

People mix up the Rapture with the Book of Revelations.

275. Mother Teresa was extremely religious.
Mother Teresa was an atheist. This wasn't known until after her death. She writes about it many times in her letters. She had a belief in God, but after years of being surrounded by the poverty-stricken and the dying, her faith sadly waned.

She couldn't publicly admit it because she had raised millions for charity. She went to her grave with people believing her to be one of the most devout Christians in the world.

276. Rastafarians call themselves "Rastafarians."
"Rastafarian" is not a derogatory term. They just don't like any labels, good or bad, because

labels can be corrupted and cause separation with anyone who is different. To say someone has the right religion or belief is to imply that someone else has the wrong one. So they would prefer to live without labels.

277. Witch doctors stick pins into voodoo dolls to place curses on people.

This is not a belief in any version of voodoo in Ghana and Benin. Nor does cannibalism or resurrection have anything to do with voodoo. Voodoo is conceptually about healing the body and eradicating spirits from the human body. Even the Catholic Church accepts voodoo as a healthy and peaceful religion.

Some voodoo beliefs use a doll called a poppet that has peg-holes in certain places. Twigs are inserted into the holes to drive out spirits, not needles. The whole idea of voodoo being evil became popularized by the James Bond movie, Live and Let Die.

SCIENCE

278. Raindrops looks like tear drops.
　　Some people believe that raindrops are spherical but this is also untrue. Raindrops are shaped like a hamburger bun.

279. Sucking a penny will fool an alcohol Breathalyzer.
　　That sounds so stupid, it just might be true. But it isn't.

280. The Richter scale is used to measure earthquakes.
　　The Richter scale hasn't been used in about forty years.
　　The MMS (Moment Magnitude Scale) has been used since the 1970s.

281. Toilets flush the opposite way in the Southern Hemisphere because of the Coriolis force.
　　The Coriolis force only applies to huge forces of water or wind like a hurricane or whirlpool. A toilet is too small to be affected.

282. All metals are magnetic.
　　Only four metals are magnetic – nickel, iron, gadolinium, and cobalt.

283. Louise Brown was the first test tube baby.

Despite the fact that this is what the newspapers said, Brown was created in a petri dish.

284. Water is clear, not blue.

Water is blue. It is extremely faint, but it is irrefutably blue.

285. Steam comes out of a hot shower.

"Misty water" isn't necessarily steam. Steam can only be formed when water boils. But steam itself is nearly twice as hot as boiling water. That steam-like water vapor you see in the shower doesn't have a definitive name.

286. The North Star is the brightest star in the sky.

Sirius is the brightest star in the sky. The North Star (or Polaris to use its official name) seems the brightest because it's easier to notice as it is in the center of a constellation.

287. Air is mostly made of oxygen.

Teenagers are more likely to know this than adults. 78% of the air we breathe is nitrogen. Only 21% of it is oxygen.

288. Glass is the most viscous liquid in the world.

This false statement comes from the idea that old houses have windows where the glass at the bottom seems to droop as if the glass is gradually pouring down. But that "pouring down" substance is good old fashioned grime.

Glass, however is even stranger than that because it is not solid OR a liquid. Glass is a fourth state of matter known as "amorphous solid."

"Four states? " you may ask. "But there's only three states of matter..." Eh….

289. There are three states of matter – solid, liquid, gas.

You might be thinking there are four states of matter including amorphous solid. But there are actually sixteen (for now.)

The other eleven types of matter are – plasma, superfluid, super solid, strange matter, strong symmetric matter, weak symmetric matter, disordered hyperuniformity, quark-gluon plasma, neutronium, degenerate matter, fermionic condensate, and Bose-Einstein condensate.

Sometimes, even I hate science.

290. Atoms look like a nucleus with electrons spinning around it.

Even with the most advanced technology, we still have a small understanding of what atoms look like. Electrons don't spin around the nucleus like the Earth spins around the Sun. Their movements are more erratic.

It's impossible to draw an atom accurately. 99.9999% of an atom is empty space. If an atom was the size of a football stadium, the nucleus would be the size of a fly in the center. There is no possible way you can scale this on a diagram.

291. Atoms are the smallest things in the universe.

Most people know that the proton and neutron that make up the nucleus of the atom are smaller. The edges of atoms are covered with even smaller particles called electrons.

But neutrinos are far smaller. Neutrinos are subatomic particles with no electric mass. (If you don't know what that means....neither do I.)

They are so small, that if an atom was the size of the Solar System, a neutrino would be the size of a golf ball.

292. The more chromosomes an animal has, the more complex and intelligent it is.

Human beings have very few chromosomes compared to other animals. We have a total of forty-six.

The organism with the most is one of the first living things; the fern with 1,260. The amount of chromosomes an organism has gives no indication of its complexity.

293. Copper is the best conductor.

Copper is an excellent conductor but it is the most commonly used because it's far cheaper than silver, which is the best conductor.

294. If something is radioactive, it glows.

Radiation isn't the same as radioactivity. Radioactivity is naturally invisible. All living things are traced in radioactivity and it is harmless.

Radiation is how energy such as heat, radio waves, and X-Rays travel in space at nearly the speed of light.

Radiation is always dangerous in large doses e.g. infrared from the sun and ultraviolet rays from a sunbed can both give you cancer in the long run.

So what glows? Radium. So to be clear, radiation, radioactivity, and radium are different things. Radium is the only radioactive element that glows but ONLY if it has contact with paint.

Once it was discovered that it was lethal, people automatically associated any science word that begins with *Rad* with glowing and death.

295. Coins have a weird metallic smell.

That smell isn't the coins; it's you.

When human perspiration mixes with the iron of a coin, it creates a distinct smell that people say smells like "metal." If a coin has never had contact with human skin, this smell will not exist. You get a similar smell when blood comes into contact with skin because blood contains iron.

296. The genes in redheads are going extinct.

I have heard this said about blondes too. Neither are true.

SHAKESPEARE

That's right. Shakespeare gets his own chapter. Deal with it.

297. Actors spoke in a "Shakespeare voice" when performing Shakespeare's plays.

John Barton is the most knowledgeable Shakespearean in the world and he says the "Shakespeare voice" is a recent invention.

At the time of Shakespeare, actors had a voice that sounded like a mix of Irish, Welsh, Northern English, and Scottish.

Rather than the clipped, booming voices of Patrick Stewart or Ian McKellen, actors sounded like drunken pirates.

298. Shakespeare was just a writer.

Not only was William Shakespeare an actor, but he acted throughout his entire writing career. The part he played most was The Ghost in Hamlet.

299. William Shakespeare spelt his name as "William Shakespeare."

Shakespeare never spelt his name that way nor did he spell it the same way twice in all of the existing copies of his signature. His signatures include – Willm Shakspere, William Shakspeare,

William Shakespe, William Shakspere, Willm Shaksp, Wm Shakspe.

300. William Shakespeare wrote lots of posh and fancy plays.

One of my classmates asked my Shakespeare teacher, "Who would be the modern version of Shakespeare?"

His answer was, "Eminem."

Shakespeare was a genius when it came to creating words and rhythm. Eminem is so good with rhythm and language that he made words rhyme with orange just to prove that he could.

But it's not just because of Eminem's skill; it's his radical lyrics.

Twenty years ago, one swearword could guarantee an 18 rating for a movie. Nowadays it is rare because we have become desensitized to violence and vulgar language.

So how do you think people reacted 400 years ago when Shakespeare characters killed, mutilated, decapitated, and cannibalized each other? "Nut-hookers," "flax-wrenches," "scullions," "rampallians," "lewdsters," and "fustilarians" sound silly now but back then, these words would be considered filthy.

Shakespeare's plays were like a fusion of Tarantino and South Park in terms of vulgarity.

Audiences had never seen vulgarity like this before on stage. And that's why they loved it.

301. Romeo and Juliet has the quote, "A rose by any other name smells just as sweet."

This quote is from Star Trek. This was back before people could check things on iPads in five seconds (which were also in Star Trek.)

The quote is, "That which we call a rose by any other name would smell as sweet."

302. Macbeth starts with witches saying, "Bubble, bubble boil and trouble."

The quote is, "Double double, toil and trouble."

I've studied the play in school and performed the show and even I get this wrong .

303. Romeo and Juliet were "star-crossed lovers" because they experienced true love.

Shooting stars used to be seen as an omen rather than a sign of good luck. A star crossing the sky used to signify that there would be a significant death that night.

When Romeo and Juliet was written, calling them "star-crossed lovers" was implying that their romance was doomed.

304. People understood Shakespeare back in his time.

More than half of Londoners at the time were so uneducated that they couldn't even write their name. Most of Shakespeare's audiences were peasants. They were expected to watch a play that could be over four hours long with an average of 53 new words and phrases per play.

Even the biggest Shakespeare fans of today can't understand everything.

As an experiment, the Globe in London performed Shakespeare's tragedy Troilus and Cressida with the dialogue spoken the way it sounded four centuries ago. Words like "war" were pronounced like "whaarr" and "knight," "knife," and "know" pronounced the "k."

Renowned New York Times critic, John Lahr said he understood less than a third of the show.

305. William Shakespeare created thirty-eight plays.

Shakespeare wrote three plays and copied the rest from other stories. He would read countless stories, plays, and poems and steal the core story and make it better.

The only ones that are considered his creations are – Love's Labor's Lost, The Tempest, and A Midsummer Night's Dream.

306. There is a lost play written by Shakespeare called Cardenio.

This play has been found recently. It has already been performed many times in London.

It is considered to be one Shakespeare's strongest plays in the same league as Hamlet and King Lear.

307. The most popular Shakespeare play of his time was Hamlet.

Shakespeare's most famous play in his time was King John.

If you haven't heard of it, that's because it is the least performed Shakespeare play nowadays.

308. Shakespeare invented the most words in the English language.

Writer of Paradise Lost, John Milton has created the most English words. Milton invented 630 words including "pandemonium", "terrific", and "healthy".

It is said that Shakespeare invented thousands of words. This is an oversimplification.

Shakespeare created 2,035 words AND phrases. He concocted sayings like "in a pickle" "the be-all and end-all" and "knock, knock, who's there?" Shakespeare created these phrases but he only created 229 words like "bubble", "eyeball", and "wormhole". Most of his words like "pumpion", "varlot", and "moldwarp" never caught on. Most of Milton's words are still used today.

Shakespeare's 2,000+ phrases is staggering but Milton devised three times as many words as the Elizabethan author.

TECHNOLOGY

309. We should use the conventional QWERTY keyboard.

Look at your nearest keyboard. You will notice that the first few letters are QWERTY. This is the "normal" type of keyboard. Sadly, it is terribly outdated. The QWERTY typewriter wasn't invented to make people type fast but to type slowly so the keys wouldn't jam.

So if this is the slow way, we should use the fast keyboard, right?

But that means we have to unlearn how we type and learn the new way. Imagine if everyone in the world had to learn a new alphabet. Imagine if scientists guaranteed us it was better than our alphabet. Would you want to switch?

People don't like change. For this sort of thing, it can only work if everyone agrees to change and I don't see how that's possible.

310. If a plane is about to crash, the survival rate is very low.

I was talking to a friend today and her mother was in a plane crash. Quite a horrific one too. She was beside the window and she saw the wing literally rip off. The plane crashed violently and tragically, there were fatalities. Of 200 people, do you know how many people died? Two.

From 1983 to 2000, there have been 53,487 people in plane crashes in America. 2,280 died. That's less than 4%. Any deaths are horrible but a plane is not the deathtrap people expect it to be. People's paranoia's have been warped by television and movies rather than statistics and the news.

311. If a door burst open on a plane, the compression would tear the aircraft apart.

This haunting image has been popularized because of the movie Final Destination where a plane rips open after an explosion on the flight. If a window or a door were to open on a plane, it would cause a bit of suction but it would revert to normal after a few seconds.

Nobody would get sucked out like the movie Goldfinger unless you were right beside the door or window straight after it opened.

312. People in the 1950s believed that in the future, there would only be five computers worldwide.

It was rumored that Thomas Watson, the Chairman of IBM said this. This is false. Even if it was true, you have to remember the first computer weighed thirty tons. Ten years later, they were still over a ton. People back then couldn't imagine society of today whipping out 2,000 pound iPad's to play Angry Birds.

313. Apple Macs can't get viruses.
Viruses on Macs are rare but Microsoft Word and Excel and other similar documents can be corrupted.

314. Online dating sites are filled with sleazy, socially inept creeps.
Statistically, the most common job that a person has in an online-dating site is a teacher.

315. The police need to keep a criminal on the phone as long as possible to trace the call.
It takes seconds for 911 systems to trace a call.

316. E-Cigarettes are a good substitute for cigarettes.
Anything is better than cigarettes but e-cigarettes are not as great as you would believe. The idea behind them is that you get the buzz from the nicotine but there is no tar so it can't cause damage to your lungs.

But e-cigarettes contain formaldehyde and acetone, which can cause eye disorders, respiratory problems, and cancer. Side effects from e-cigarettes may be more common than real cigarettes. Over 200 reports occur a month in the US that involve children being ill or poisoned from the vapor from the e-cigarettes.

317. Dropping a toaster in a bathtub full of water would kill you.

It might blow a fuse and you can say goodbye to having toast the next day (unless you know a good café) but it won't kill you. You won't even feel a shock.

318. Turn the sound off on an iPhone to save battery.

An iPhone actually uses MORE battery without sound! When your phone rings, instead of making sound, it vibrates. The amount of kinetic energy needed to make your phone move requires far more effort than sound energy.

319. Wikipedia isn't a reliable source of information.

Over the years, Wikipedia has been drastically updated. The site is far stricter with updated information.

Wikipedia is now considered to be one of the most reliable sources of information on the Internet to the point where it's perfectly acceptable to quote Wikipedia in court.

320. It's dangerous to use a cellphone near a gas station.

There has never been an example of cellphones causing any potential harm at a gas station nor is there any scientific basis for this claim.

321. You can hack computers in seconds.

Despite what movies like Mission Impossible show you, hacking usually requires a lot of trial and error and can take hours, sometimes days.

322. An Electromagnetic Pulse (EMP) shuts down all electronics rendering everything inert.

Movies like The Matrix Revolutions, Escape From LA, and The Day the Earth Stood Still show an EMP disabling all electronics instantly.

Even news reports scare viewers with the possibility that a solar flare from the sun could hit Earth, devastating all technology, which would send us back to the Stone Age.

If an EMP came from a solar flare or from a manmade device, electronics like televisions or cars might stop working briefly but they will be back to normal within a few minutes. The worst-case scenario from an EMP is that some of the power grid would have to be replaced. No single incident could disable all technology worldwide.

323. If you put sugar into a gas tank, it will destroy a car's engine.

If this was true, people would do this all of the time out of revenge. But sugar doesn't caramelize and so it doesn't affect the fuel.

So you have to find another way to get back at your enemies (I recommend a stern telling-off.)

324. The Amish don't use electricity.

The Amish community use solar power, artificial light, and batteries for their washing machines, medicine, business, and even for their kitchen appliances.

325. Elevators can collapse if one of the cables snaps.

Elevators have four cables keeping them up. If three got cut, one cable would be strong enough to maintain the weight of the elevator.

If somehow, all the cables snapped, the automatic brakes would kick in stopping the elevator from falling.

It's impossible for an elevator to collapse unless there was some natural disaster demolishing the entire building like an earthquake or a hurricane. An elevator will never fall apart because of some random fault like you've seen in so many horror movies.

326. A DNA analysis takes a couple of minutes.
Genes are astronomically complicated. The most advanced Genetic Analyzer in the world will take over 12 hours to analyze DNA.

327. A plane's black box is black.
It used to be but they changed it to orange in 1965 so it was easier to find after a plane crash because its color stood out more.

VIDEO GAMES

328. The most successful video game ever is Super Mario Bros.

Super Mario Bros is the third most successful game. It was second for the longest time but was recently beaten by Wii Sports. However, the most successful video game ever is Tetris with over 170 million copies sold.

329. The Tetris theme song is just a video game song.

This song is an Old Russian folk tune called Korobeiniki. It is over a century old but it will forever be immortalized as "The Tetris Theme Song."

330. When old video games didn't work, you would just blow into the cartridge and it would work fine.

Blowing into a video game cartridge does what is known in scientific terms as "absolutely nothing." Your childhood was a lie.

331. Video games have no purpose in the real world.

People are nine times better at absorbing information if it is visually simulated rather than reading it.

Exercise-based games have been proven to help the elderly, especially those with Parkinson's.

Modern shoot-em-ups develop multi-tasking skills. Shooting and evading enemies makes your mind learn how to deal with several tasks simultaneously.

Video games develop the "precision" part of your brain, which is used in delicate jobs like surgery. Surgeons who played games were 37% less prone to errors and 27% faster than those who didn't.

Video games have millions of colors compared to a few hundred colors decades ago. This helps younger children develop their cerebral cortex enabling them to decipher color shades.

332. Donkey Kong was an obvious mistranslation. He should have been called Monkey Kong.

Shigeru Miyamoto, the creator of Donkey Kong knew that calling a person "an ass" in English was an insult meaning they were stupid. Since Kong is a reference to King Kong, Miyamoto assumed Kong's name translated as Stupid Ape.

He did not know that ass also meant "donkey" nor did he know donkey and monkey sounded similar in English. It was coincidence.

333. Nintendo is about thirty years old.
   Nintendo is over a century old. The company started in 1889 by producing handmade playing cards. In the 1960s, it veered into the toy industry and eventually, the video game industry in the 1970s.

334. Space Invaders ships intentionally get faster as you progress through the game.
   If there is too much information on a screen at once, the computer will lag and slow down. How the ships move at the end of a level is how they should've moved at the start. They get faster because every time a ship is destroyed, there is less data on the screen. It was never intentional.
   The designers were frustrated by this design flaw but players assumed the game was adapting to their skill and it helped make the game the most successful video games of its time. Now every video game in the world has the "difficulty learning curve" and Space Invaders invented it by accident.

335. Pong was the first video game ever.
   The first video game was Tennis for Two and it was invented in 1958 by Michael Higinbotham.
   Pong was created in 1972 and was the first game that could be played at home when it was imported to the Atari console in 1975.

WAR

336. War is worse than ever.
Unsurprisingly, World War II accounts for the most deaths in war.

This had far more deaths than the wars in Afghanistan, Korea, Vietnam, or Kuwait combined. Annually, the Iraq War had about a hundred thousand deaths in the past decade.

That may sound horrific, but it can't compare to nearly twenty million people PER YEAR during WW2.

337. If a Gettysburg statue of a man on horseback has all of the horse's legs on the ground, it means the man fought in a battle and survived.

If the horse has one leg up, it means the man died from his wounds after the battle.

If the horse has its front legs up, it means the man died in battle.

Eh…..no.

338. The Zulus used primitive weapons.
The movie, Zulu shows the tribe fighting with spears and shields against the rifles of the English. In reality, the Zulus killed entire battalions in spite of their inferior weaponry thanks to their great numbers. The Zulus were

observant and understood that the English possessed far superior weaponry. They stole most of the guns from those they kidnapped and used them in battle.

339. The 100 Years War lasted 100 years.

The only thing worse than a boring historic title is a boring AND inaccurate historic title. The 100 Years War lasted 116 years.

340. 300 Spartans fought a million Persians.

As hard as it is to believe, the movie 300 is not historically accurate.

7,000 people from Greece (including 300 Spartans) fought against 180,000 Persians.

341. Samurais used swords.

Samurais saw swords as a last resort. They believed it required no skill. A bow and arrow was the real weapon of a samurai. Drawing a sword carried a stigma because it implied that the samurai was too lazy to use his bow.

342. Samurais were the most efficient killers in Ancient Japan.

Japanese infantry nearly always won wars. Samurais are better remembered because they look really cool.

People have this idea that samurais never ran from battle. They did. If they knew they were going to lose, they had no choice.

Despite what the movie, The Last Samurai depicts, samurais rarely took their own lives by stabbing themselves with their own swords. Emperors discouraged it because they relied on as many men in their army as possible.

WEAPONS

343. **Sword fights are portrayed accurately in movies.**

In the movie, Kill Bill, The Bride fights a group called the Crazy 88. This is a battle no one could win and it has nothing to do with skill. A sword becomes less sharp with every strike. After using it on ten people, the sword would be coated in so much blood (and entrails) that even the sharpest blade would become as effective as wooden stick.

Swords can easily break after only a few strikes. In real sword fights, Vikings and pirates did everything in their power to ensure their swords never collided to avoid breaking them.

344. **A nuclear bomb looks like a huge missile.**

When people think of a nuke, they probably think of the missile that Kong rides like a horse in the film, Dr. Strangelove or the atomic bomb that the mutants worship in the movie, Beneath the Planet of the Apes. The nuke used in World War 2 was a six-foot tall sphere, covered in hundreds of cable wires. It looked like a random piece of machinery or an extremely old computer. You would have no idea it was a weapon, not to mention capable of killing hundreds of thousands of people in mere seconds.

345. Hundreds of years ago, arguments were settled in a duel to the death.

The last duel was as recent as 1967. It was between two politicians in France called Gaston Deffere and Rene Ribiere. Deffere complained that Ribiere was fidgeting too much in mid-debate and so Ribiere challenged him to a duel.

No one died but that doesn't make it less ridiculous.

346. You can't tell if a gun is empty or not.

How many movies have you seen where the bad guy is given an empty gun and he believes it's full? Bullets are metal. Metal is heavy. A gun with no bullets is noticeably lighter than a gun with a full clip. It's pretty easy to tell the difference between a handgun with no bullets or with one bullet.

347. If you shoot the tank of a car, it will explode.

This is a myth made famous from movies. You would need to shoot a car with exceptional precision, which will vary from car to car, tank to tank, gun to gun. There is no magical spot on all automobiles that makes them explode.

WORDS

348. The creator of the Cat in the Hat, Dr Seuss pronounced his name as "Soose."
Dr Theodor Geisel's pseudonym Dr. Seuss is pronounced "See-oice."He wanted it to rhyme with "rejoice."

Also, he HATED kids. Yet he wrote kids books. For some reason.

349. "Ye" is a medieval word that was the plural for "you."
When the printing press was invented, they had a marking for each letter; A for A, B for B, etc.

They had a few extra symbols for certain sounds like of "ch," "sh," and "th."

The "th" symbol looked like a fancy "y." So the symbol for "the" would look like "ye." So words like "ye people" meant "the people" but readers assumed "ye" was a plural word.

350. "Snapshot" is slang for a quick camera picture.
It was originally a hunting term that meant, "to fire at a fast-moving target without aiming properly."

351. Sushi translates to "Raw fish."
It means, "sour rice."

352. "Adam" means first man.

If a character is the first of his kind, people tend to name them "Adam." Even Frankenstein's Monster is sometimes called Adam.

"Adam" is most famously referencing Adam in the Garden of Eden.

Adam meant "to have blood in one's face." The blood shows that Adam is alive because God breathed life into him. The name "Adam" signifies that he is alive, not that he is the first of his kind.

353. "Decimate" means destroy.

Decimation was a punishment in Ancient Rome where one in ten men were killed. "Decimate" means destroying 10% of something.

354. "Hello" is a universal greeting.

"Hello" was said as a way to express a nice surprise. When the phone was first invented, conversations would go like this –

Man 1: Who's this?

Man 2: It's John.

Man 1: Hello John! Lovely to hear from you!

That seems normal but he's not saying "hello" as a greeting. He's saying it because he now acknowledges the person he is talking to is his friend John. So "hello" was said often as a reassuring surprise until it eventually became part of every conversation.

355. "Ultimate" means the best.

"Ultimate" was a Latin word that meant "the last one."

However I will use it in the right context by saying this misconception is the ultimate fact in this chapter.

The Ten Most Bizarre Misconceptions

356. Rats caused the Black Death.
No, and it wasn't fleas either.

It was squirrels. Marmot squirrels from Mongolia gradually spread the disease, as they are extremely prone to the bubonic plague. They spread the parasite to fleas and rats and eventually humans.

Technically they've killed more humans than any animal on Earth apart from mosquitos with a death toll of over one billion.

357. Einstein concocted the Big Bang Theory, the General Theory of Relativity, the concept of atom structure and parallel universes.
All of these theories were invented by the same person who, bizarrely wasn't a scientist – the poet, Edger Allan Poe.

Most famous for writing The Tell-Tale Heart, The Pit and the Pendulum, and The Raven, he wrote all of these theories in Eureka, his final poem in 1848 just before he died in a gutter.

358. Doctors know how anesthetic works.
This is what people believe – you receive an anesthetic which paralyses, impairs, or deactivates the section of the brain that receives stimulus to indicate pain.

But there is no single section of the brain that alerts us with pain. Our ancestors have known for years that certain painkillers like morphine and penicillin relieve us of pain but they didn't know how. You'd think doctors of today would have a biological understanding but it still remains a mystery. The brain is far from being understood.

359. You are mostly you.
.........wait, what? What does that mean? What else would I be made of?

Bacteria. You are made up of one trillion human cells but you have ten times more bacteria. You are basically a petri dish in shoes.

360. Halitosis exists.
Listerine is the company who invented the mouthwash you use for halitosis.

They invented something else – halitosis.

The mouthwash was used as an antiseptic but it didn't sell well. Then it was used as a floor cleaner but it didn't make a profit.

Then it was used as mouthwash for a disorder they made up. The mouthwash is identical now to when it was used as an antiseptic. Some people have bad breath but it's not a condition or a disorder. It's like saying having an itchy head is a disorder. It's not. You just have an itchy head.

361. No one knows what makes people gay.

The template of a human fetus is female. Six to eight weeks after conception, the fetus is blasted with androgens (male hormones), which will decide if the fetus will be male or female.

A second dose of androgens occurs after another six to eight weeks. This dosage will decide the fetus' sexual orientation.

A fetus with a small amount of androgens will keep it female and another small amount of androgens will give the fetus a female-structured brain.

A fetus with a large amount of androgens will turn it male and another large amount of androgens will give the fetus a male-structured brain.

However, as a pregnancy advances, complications can happen. Stress, anxiety, diet, physical health, exercise, and even the weather can alter a pregnant woman's hormones (and her androgens.)

So if a fetus receives a lot of male hormones and becomes male, it may not receive enough androgens later because of complications and it may be left with a female structured brain.

It's rare for the first dose to be less than the second because complications tend to happen as the pregnancy progress, which is why there are statistically fewer lesbians than gay men.

362. In the UK, you can drink alcohol when you are eighteen.

You can drink alcohol in the UK when you are five.

And no, you didn't misread that. In the UK, you are not allowed to consume alcohol until you are eighteen <u>*at the bar.*</u>

It is completely legal for someone else to buy you alcohol if you are underage and you can consume it in your home so long as you are five or older.

But not four years old…because that would just be stupid.

363. Evolution is too slow to observe accurately.

Elephants are not as commonly killed as before because they are evolving without tusks. If an elephant is tuskless, it is useless to a poacher. So the absence of tusks guarantees its survival.

Skinks used to lay eggs but now they give birth.

Pepper moths were white but now, they are nearly all black.

Since Asian crabs have been introduced to Europe, mussels in the UK have developed harder shells to survive.

Even human evolution can be observed. The Sherpa of Nepal (the group who helped people climb Mt Everest) can survive living 13,000 feet high. 2,000 feet make people feel dizzy and ill. No one can survive 13,000 feet for very long except the Sherpa who live there. This is the fastest human evolution on record. They've only been living there for 3,000 years.

364. Eating lots of fruit is healthy.

Fruit has a lot of sugar called fructose. It's fruit sugar but sugar nonetheless. Excessive sugar is bad no matter what food it comes from.

It's common for older people to have a health scare so they decide to be super healthy and replace all of their old vices and addictions with a lot of fruit.

This sounds like a good idea. Instead of a beer, have a smoothie. But if you introduce a huge quantity of sugar into your body suddenly, it can spike your insulin levels.

People may have a health scare, start eating fruit, and ironically give themselves pancreatic cancer. Pancreatic cancer is common in the elderly but it's not because they are getting old, it's because they are introducing too much sugar in their body.

That sounds a bit farfetched but Steve Jobs died of pancreatic cancer and he ate nothing but fruit.

Ashton Kutcher played him in the movie Jobs and replicated his fruit diet. A few weeks later, he had to be hospitalized after nearly giving himself pancreatic cancer (which almost never happens in a person's thirties.)

Many people believe Bill Hicks died from lung cancer or liver cancer because he smoked, drank and did drugs excessively. But he quit everything near the end of his life, started eating healthy, then died a year later from pancreatic cancer.

Fruit should be in your daily diet but don't overload your body with it.

And the final misconception is....

365. All of these facts are true.

I mentioned earlier in my book that the oldest battery discovered was from 200 BC.

But what happens if we find out that it was a fake? Or what if we find a battery from 1,000 BC?

Some facts are constantly changing. The number of moons Jupiter has changes every few years as it keeps absorbing more moons into its gravity.

Some facts change out of convenience like the way we have eight planets now just to make the Solar System diagram more convenient.

Some facts change because of technicalities. I mentioned in my last book that George Washington is the first American president due to a technicality.

The movie Jurassic World will be coming out this year. Historians discovered that dinosaurs had feathers two years after the movie Jurassic Park was released. Do you think the director is going to change the appearance of the dinosaurs to make them look realistic?

Of course not. Because it will ruin our childhood. Audience's wouldn't like it because it's different. We believe what we like or what's convenient, not the truth.

In my first book, I mentioned that Nikola Tesla discovered superior electricity to Thomas Edison. But Edison's electricity was used because he used bullying tactics and insisted his was superior. If we used Nikola Tesla form of electricity, technology would have leapt ahead fifty years. That arrogance set us back half a century.

This is why we cannot reject the truth. No matter how much we want to be right, the purpose of knowledge is to allow us to leap forward as a species.

If you dismiss anything in this book, then research it. You might be right. You might be wrong. I might be wrong. There is no shame in being wrong. There is shame in following an idea blindly. Questioning ideas is not a bad thing. It helps us understand them better. That constant questioning is how we got to where we are today.

There is no shame in not knowing. There is shame in not finding out.